Leader's guide

EXAMINATION

the key idea

Cross Examination is designed with the average young person in mind. And of course there is no such thing as an average young person! They are all special and unique.

The ideas in this course can be found in the *Christianity Explained* course for adults devised by the Rev. Michael Bennett.

The course is based on three simple features:

1. Young people will respond to the Christian faith when they have the opportunity to look at it without being pushed or manipulated.

2. The majority of young people in western countries do not have even the most basic understanding of what the Christian faith is about. Ask them about Jesus Christ and you get a strange variety of responses!

3. Christian faith grows best in an environment of friendliness, friendship, non-judging exploration and straight-forward 'non-churchy' explanation.

The evangelism which takes place through this package is based on learning and exploration over six sessions rather than the power of a one-off event or an emotional moment. For this reason, any conversions or faith decisions are likely to be more considered, permanent and life changing.

HOW to Get the Best value out of Cross Examination

The course is flexible and can be used in schools' work, holiday camps, confirmation classes, youth work and special local outreach events.

Certainly *Cross Examination* is a pre-planned teaching program. But it's more than that. Its great value is that an environment can be created where young people can talk about how they feel about faith and can ask their hard questions.

This is also a chance for them to come face-to-face with Jesus Christ. Many young people would not otherwise be likely to explore the data in Mark's Gospel first hand nor talk about it at all in an open atmosphere. This has to be a big plus for the Gospel!

Although the course is flexible, the focus is single and simple. There is only one major point in each session and the vocabulary is more straightforward than specially religious. Presenters should feel free to adapt the material here and there so that it fits neatly into the local circumstances, their own style and the particular characteristics of the group.

One positive factor for many young people is the limited time frame of the course. They only need to commit themselves for six or seven sessions. There is an end in view. Other kinds of courses and groups can be begun after this one, but the young people in the group know there is a limit to their commitment at this stage.

The sessions can be arranged in a relaxing way. Food and drinks can set the tone. Choose a time which suits local lifestyles and events. Breakfast sessions work well, so do late night supper parties.

The leader of the group can have a very significant role in the lives of the young people if he or she remembers four important factors:

1. **Be open.** Allow the group members to talk about the things that are on their mind. Keep a balance between your planned teaching program and the real but unexpected questions, statements and experiences which come up from the group. Don't be rigid in your planning.

2. **Be honest.** If you don't know the answer to a question, admit it and offer to think about it, research it and come back to it again at the start of the next session. Be prepared to admit that some of the world's toughest questions do not have black and white or clear-cut answers.

3. **Be sensitive.** Anyone can get decisions by pouring on some kind of manipulative heat. Be straight with the group members. Give them time to think while encouraging them not to avoid reviewing their lives.

4. **Be passionate.** While being open, honest and sensitive, still let your own love for God and your concern for the young people show through. They should know that these things matter to you.

When all is said and done, however, we must remember that this is **just** a course. Words on a page. Ideas that can be discussed. There is no magic here! New life is the work of the Holy Spirit. It is this Spirit who works to change people's attitudes, who helps them to be open to the truth of the Gospel of Jesus and who fosters germination of the Gospel seed which has been planted.

Let's pray that this Spirit will be working in your group as you embark on leading your *Cross Examination* course.

intRODucing cross Examination to YOUR GROUP

You may wish to begin the course with a preliminary session or you could combine this with Session A, maybe commencing with pizza and coke as a way of setting up a relaxed environment.

Try a warming up activity which includes light-hearted introductions all round.

Explain that the purpose of *Cross Examination* is to provide a chance to seriously consider the Christian faith in a non-threatening and non-pressured way.

Reassure the group that no one will be made to look stupid or asked to do anything embarrassing. Some of the young people may have seen TV pictures of people doing strange things in Christian meetings and they may feel awkward about praying or talking about religious matters.

Remember, these sessions are exploratory and meant to be open-ended. It is not necessary to open or close the sessions with prayer. You can do your praying at home and invite other Christian friends to support you in prayer as you lead the group.

Furthermore, many teenagers are uncomfortable with reading books aloud. They may struggle to do it well — especially with an unfamiliar book like the Bible. It is best to avoid asking them to do this.

Bible for Beginners

The Bible is no ordinary book. Actually it's a whole collection of books all stuck together between two covers. Some people read the Bible by starting at the front cover and keeping going. It's probably better to start at the easier key bits. Then read the rest later. We will start with Mark's Gospel in the New Testament.

Have a look inside your Bible now. Maybe you only have the New Testament half. That's OK. It's best to start there anyway.

To find your way around, first get acquainted with the Contents or Index page in the front of your Bible. Then it's a cinch.

Christians use a shorthand system to find their way around the Bible. This is how it works:

Mark 1:21
That's Mark chapter 1 verse 21

Or **Mark 1:21-28**
That's Mark chapter 1 verses 21 to 28.

Got it?

Try these simple driving tests to see how you go:

1. On what page does the New Testament begin in your Bible? Page ....

2. How many books in the New Testament are named after People? ....

3. Who wrote the last book of the Bible? (See Revelation 1:1-3) ....

4. Everyone knows the Christmas story. Or do they? Where was Jesus born? (See Luke 2:4-7) ....

5. More Christmas details. How many wise men were there? Be careful of this one! (See Matthew 2:1-2) ....

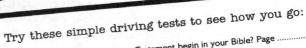

2

The warm up exercise on page 2 of the work book (reproduced here) is merely to give people practice at finding their way around the Bible. Make sure everyone has the same version of the Bible and get them to handle it a lot during this segment. Make sure they know where the index is and how to use it. Explain references.

If you have the time, introduce the group to different versions, pointing out the value of modern versions like the **Good News Bible** or the **Contemporary English Version**. There is no need to struggle with 'thees', 'thous', 'doests', 'whatsoevers' and 'it came to passes' these days!

Briefly introduce the four Gospels, showing them to be four stories about Jesus, by people who knew him. As eyewitness stories, they show slight variations, depending on the viewpoint of the writer and who they were written for.

Introduce Mark and encourage the group members to make themselves familiar with his Gospel. You could mention Mark's embarrassing moment! (It is probably Mark who is mentioned in the story of Jesus' arrest. See Mark 14:50-52.) After Jesus' death and resurrection, Mark's home became a meeting place for the Christians. See Acts 12:12. Later on he probably worked with Peter to write the story of Jesus which we now have.

Invite the group members to read several chapters of Mark between the group sessions. Encourage them to note down their surprises and discoveries and to bring to the next session any questions they may have.

You will be encouraged by the inclusion in this Leader's Guide of a section 'Top Twenty Questions — the most asked questions about Mark's Gospel', prepared by Michael Bennett, the author of *Christianity Explained*. (See page 41)

Jesus in charge

AIM

The object of this first study is to introduce group members to the man Jesus as he is described in Mark's Gospel. We look at his authority and miracles which point to his status as God's Son.

This session explores what it means that Jesus is the Son of God. He is seen as a person with a unique kind of **authority** — the authority of God his Father.

SESSION NOTES

In **Section 1** ('What I think about Jesus') it is important to emphasise that there are no right or wrong answers. Encourage the group members to write down some of the things they know about Jesus and what they think about him.

In **Section 2** we focus on Jesus' authority as different from the other 'professional' teachers around. It was not just that he was the exorciser of one particular evil spirit, but that he had a kind of in-built authority in what he said and over evil spirits in general (verse 27).

Here is an example of Jesus healing a crippled man. The Bible tells the stories of about 30 instances like this. The sick, the blind, the paralysed were healed and even dead people were brought back to life.

Jesus' authority to forgive sins shows him to have the same authority as God. The Bible describes him as God's son — equal with God. He is a very special God-man — God and human in the same personality.

The coming of Jesus to the earth is like God the Creator visiting his creation. God is in charge of everything. And Mark's Gospel says that this is exactly the same for Jesus. Because Jesus is really God in a human form, he forgives sin, like God himself.

When Jesus asked people to leave their work and join his team, they seemed to respond immediately and were drawn by his invitation and authority. Two thousand years later, we are invited also to join his team.

continued page 11.

SESSION A

jesus in charge

1. What I think about Jesus

Have you heard anything about Jesus?

....
....
....

What do you think of him?

....
....

2. Jesus in charge — as a teacher

Read Mark 1:21-28

At what were the people amazed? (v.22)

He taught with authority, not like the teachers of the Law of Moses

Religious leaders taught the ancient laws from the times of Moses. The people noticed that Jesus' teaching was different. In what ways?

He seemed to have more authority than the teachers

How would you describe the man with an evil spirit in him?

He was out of control

How did Jesus show his authority in this situation?

He forced the evil spirit to obey him.

3

3. Jesus in charge — over sickness

Read Mark 2:1-12

Why were the four men so determined to get the paralysed man to Jesus?

They were sure Jesus could help their friend and they didn't want to miss out.

What did Jesus see as the paralysed man's greatest need?

Forgiveness.

Jesus said, 'Your sins are forgiven.' What do you think sins are?

The things we do wrong.

What did Jesus see as more important — to forgive the man's sin or to heal him?

To forgive the man.

Why do you think that was so?

Perhaps this would help him more deeply and bring change to his attitude and outlook.

Over what two areas does Jesus have authority?

Forgiving sin and healing sickness.

In forgiving sins, what was Jesus claiming?

He had the same authority as God.

4. Jesus in charge — over people

Read Mark 1:16-20

In this passage we see Jesus walking up to people and commanding them to leave their jobs and families.

How did they respond?

They did it straightaway.

What does this show you about Jesus' authority?

He convinced and attracted people in powerful ways.

Who do you say Jesus is?

- ✦ 'He's a liar so I should ignore him.'
- ✦ 'He's a lunatic so I'd better keep away from him.'
- ✦ 'He's Lord so I'll begin to serve him.'

4

This means coming into line with his authority, like players responding to their captain and coach. God — and Jesus — is in charge of very powerful things in the world he made. However, it is dangerously possible to resist and avoid his authority. That's the big test for human beings of all kinds!

Invite members of the group to focus on the 'Think about' section. Do not invite responses in the group — just a period of silent thinking or encouragement to think seriously about this during the coming week.

Also invite group members to read Mark chapters 1 to 4. Suggest that they make a note of any questions they have ready for Session B.

Nailed to a cross

AIM

To show that Jesus was not just a very good teacher and healer. To show that Jesus' death and rising from death are central to what Christianity is all about, hence the title of this course — *Cross Examination* (thoroughly checking the meaning of Jesus and his execution on the cross).

SESSION NOTES

1. The warm up exercise is provided. There are no correct answers nor any need to share answers.

2. Allow time for questions arising from Mark 1 – 4. Limit the time on this so that the main theme of the session is not squeezed out. It would be unwise to give the impression that you know all the answers. Much better to convey a humble attitude which suggests the most likely answers to the questions.

3. Remind the group of the main theme emerging from Session A.

4. The second panel on this page gives group members a reminder of some of the main events leading to Jesus' death. Briefly tell the group that this kind of death was an extremely agonising one. The victim, after being nailed to the cross, was lifted up so that his feet were about a metre about the ground. His body weight was supported by the nails. To inhale he had to push up with his legs. There he was left to die by suffocation.

5. The third panel probes the meaning of the death of Christ. There is a comment on the phenomenon of the darkness in the 'Top Twenty' section of page 47. Jesus' cry in verse 34, seems so desperate. But we must face the stark reality of it. Although Jesus and his Father were one and could not be separated, in some strange way God had turned his back on the sin and evil Jesus was carrying in his death.

6. It is impossible to fully explain the meaning of the death of Christ. No explanation ties it all up completely. One attempt which has helped many people is outlined on page 29.

continued page 15.

NaiLeD to a CROSS

1. Gut reactions

Describe how you feel about the boxed issues using the symbols :

A — I'm feeling really good
B — I'm feeling okay
C — Things could be better
D — I wish you hadn't asked

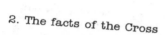

1. About my team ..... ☐
2. About my family ... ☐
3. About school/ college/work .... ☐
4. About my friends .. ☐
5. About God .... ☐
6. About the church... ☐

2. The facts of the Cross

Read Mark 14:60-65 and 15:9-41

From the following verses, list the things that happened to Jesus:

14:64-65 —

....

15:15 —

....

15:17-20 —

....

15:24 —

....
....
....

15:31 —

....
....

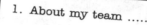

5

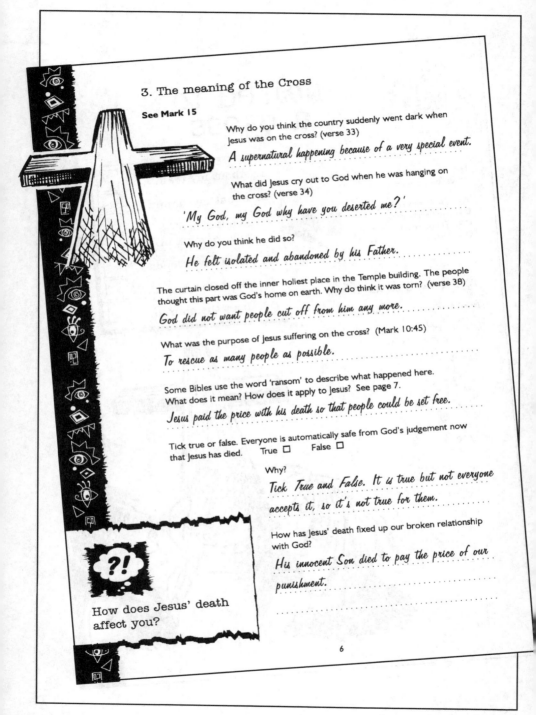

3. The meaning of the Cross

See Mark 15

Why do you think the country suddenly went dark when Jesus was on the cross? (verse 33)

A supernatural happening because of a very special event.

What did Jesus cry out to God when he was hanging on the cross? (verse 34)

'My God, my God why have you deserted me?'

Why do you think he did so?

He felt isolated and abandoned by his Father.

The curtain closed off the inner holiest place in the Temple building. The people thought this part was God's home on earth. Why do think it was torn? (verse 38)

God did not want people cut off from him any more.

What was the purpose of Jesus suffering on the cross? (Mark 10:45)

To rescue as many people as possible.

Some Bibles use the word 'ransom' to describe what happened here. What does it mean? How does it apply to Jesus? See page 7.

Jesus paid the price with his death so that people could be set free.

Tick true or false. Everyone is automatically safe from God's judgement now that Jesus has died.   True ☐   False ☐

Why?

Tick True and False. It is true but not everyone accepts it, so it's not true for them.

How has Jesus' death fixed up our broken relationship with God?

His innocent Son died to pay the price of our punishment.

How does Jesus' death affect you?

6

7. It would be helpful to have a picture of the layout of the Temple so that some explanation can be given about the torn curtain (verse 38). Simply described, the Temple had a larger room and a smaller room. The smaller room was the holiest part and seen as the place where God lived. The curtain separated this room from the people. Only the priest could go in on behalf of the people, and only once per year. The curtain torn from the top down emphasises that now, ordinary people could get in touch with God through the death of Jesus.

8. The picture of a 'ransom' being paid is explained on page 7 in the work book.

9. Invite group members to reflect seriously on the THINK ABOUT question. Do not invite discussion on this.

10. Encourage the group to read Mark chapters 5 – 9 before the next session.

THE GREAT RANSOM PAY UP

IF YOU DON'T PAY $1 MILLION BY MIDNIGHT, YOUR GIRLFRIEND IS DEAD MEAT!

Some translations of the Bible portray Jesus' death as a ransom. In Roman times, when important soldiers were captured by the enemy in battle they could be ransomed (bought back) if someone paid the price demanded. Kidnapping of foreigners or wealthy people still occurs today in unstable countries. Their safe return depends on payment of the ransom demanded. Again in Roman times, slaves could ransom themselves by saving enough money to purchase their freedom.

Pawn shops (called 'cash converters' these days) have existed down through the ages. People in desperate need of money pawn their valuables which can be redeemed later by paying the rate demanded by the pawnbroker.

The Bible tells us that God always had a wonderful dream about how we humans would live. He gave us guidelines to help us do it. But in our stupidity we've told him we don't need his rules. It's like we've been ambushed and captured by 'evil enemy forces'. In an incredibly generous deal, Jesus' death has become the payment for the punishment we deserve and the rescue we need. And that's why it's called a ransom.

7

BOOKed!

We are now really at the heart of our 'cross examination'. The execution of Christ was an unjust, dirty affair. But there was more to it than a cruel miscarriage of justice. The cross has become a powerful symbol and the event is seen by Christians as the pivot point of history. There is no human explanation which can fully sum up its meaning. The following concept has been prepared by the Rev. Michael Bennett, the author of *Christianity Explained*, and attempts to show the meaning of substitutionary atonement in a visual way.

You will need a large thick book, preferably not a Bible. Tell the group that this book represents the life story of any member of the group — from the day of birth (page 1) until the day of his or her death (last page).

There is no explanation which can fully sum up the meaning of the death of Christ. This is one way of looking at it.

In this book is written every time we have broken any of God's laws — every wrong deed, every wrong word, every evil thought. For example, Jesus says to hate another person is as bad as murder, according to God's outlook. To lust after another person is really a form of unfaithfulness.

Tell the group that there are many dark pages in your own book which you would not like them to read, and if they are honest, the same will be true for them also.

Hold out your left hand, palm uppermost, and say:

Now suppose this hand represents you, and let us say that the ceiling represents God. Now the Bible says that between us and God is what the Bible calls 'the charges that were against us' (Colossians 2:14). *Place the book on the upturned palm of your left hand and keep it there throughout the following explanation.*

So our sins cut us off from God. Even one blot is enough to spoil the page.

But sin is more than doing, saying or thinking wrong things. It is an attitude of rebellion against God whereby we ignore him, turn our backs on him and run our lives our own way. This is what the Bible means by *sin*. This attitude of rebellion is the motive or reason for our many *sins*.

Let me make the picture even blacker. The Bible says that, although God is love, he is also a just judge. God hates all evil and his sense of justice demands that our sin be dealt with.

So we have two problems. First, we all have much evil written in our books. Second, God judges all evil.

When we try to explain the cross, we are talking about the pivot point of history. No illustration could adequately represent this cosmic event.

Now let me try to illustrate what happened during that time Jesus was hanging on the cross. Suppose now that this hand represents Jesus. *Hold out right hand palm uppermost, the left hand with the book on it should still be held out.* Again, the ceiling represents God. Now there was no 'book' between Jesus and God. He always perfectly obeyed the will of God. He always pleased his Father.

Now in some unexplainable way, while Jesus was on the cross, God took the sins of people in every age and placed them on Jesus. *Now transfer the book from the left hand on to the upturned palm of the right hand.*

Peter put it this way: 'Christ carried the burden of our sins. He was nailed to the cross' (1 Peter 2:24) and Paul says, 'Christ never sinned! But God treated him as a sinner, so that Christ could make us acceptable to God' (2 Corinthians 5:21).

Take the idea a step further. You could say that on the cross Jesus became the most sinful man the world has ever seen, as the sins of millions and millions of believers in every age were poured into his body! Then an amazing thing happened. Remember, God is a just judge. Well, at this moment, God poured upon his own Son on the cross all the wrath and anger and punishment that should fall on the likes of you and me. You could say God executed his own Son! Jesus died of the punishment of God. To show that he had completely dealt with our sins and punishment, three days later God brought him back to life!

Now refer people back to the left hand, now empty, still with the palm uppermost.

Well, now we must ask — how much sin remains between the person who believes in Jesus, and God?

Press the point until someone answers 'none'.

So then, when a person believes in Jesus Christ, God counts him or her as acquitted and cleared of all charges. Amazing isn't it!

Go on to stress that this forgiveness is available to everyone but not automatically conferred. It is for those who accept God's grace by receiving the giver, Jesus Christ.

Alive again

AIM

To show that Jesus rose from death, a sign of his power over death, and see what this means for our lives.

SESSION NOTES

1. Allow time for questions arising from Mark 6 – 10. The common questions raised in these chapters are covered in the 'Top Twenty' section on pages 41-8.

2. Again the theme is opened up in light hearted fashion with 'Honest Abe's Acme Belief Scale'. There are no correct answers!

3. Now look at the way Jesus was able to see what would happen to him ahead of the events. This was not an isolated statement. Twice before, Jesus had pointed ahead to his death and resurrection (Mark 8:31 and 9:9-13) even using the Old Testament scriptures to reinforce his prediction. As a human he must have been uncomfortable about the prospect, even though he must have known it to be part of the divine plan for his mission.

4. Reassure the group that the records of these events in the Bible can be trusted. The New Testament talks about many witnesses meeting Jesus **after** he came alive from death. It would be extremely powerful evidence if it were heard in a court of law. And there is even supportive material in less biased non-Christian documents from the same period.

5. The Gospel of Mark stops with a brief but strong mention that Jesus came to life again. A few weeks later, when the Holy Spirit came, the followers of Jesus began spreading this good news. Read the extract from Peter's conversation with Cornelius (Acts 10:39-43). This points to the consequences of the resurrection of Jesus. One day **all** people, living and dead, will be raised. This sounds good, but it may not be.

continued page 23.

SESSION C

Alive again

Can you believe this?

1. Mark each of the following statements on a scale of 1 to 10 to show how believable they are:

HONEST ABE'S ACME BELIEF SCALE

Scale:
1 2 3 4 5 6 7 8 9 10

↑ No way José
– I wouldn't believe
this if you paid me.

In between scale.

↑ No doubt at all
– 100% right on!

Statement	Scale
Fall 10 metres without injury	1 2 3 4 5 6 7 8 9 10
Drive blindfolded without crashing	1 2 3 4 5 6 7 8 9 10
Hang-gliding is perfectly safe	1 2 3 4 5 6 7 8 9 10
Live to be 110 years old	1 2 3 4 5 6 7 8 9 10
Get 100% in a Maths exam	1 2 3 4 5 6 7 8 9 10
Cheat without ever being caught	1 2 3 4 5 6 7 8 9 10
Read the whole Bible in a day	1 2 3 4 5 6 7 8 9 10
Getting two servings of dessert at dinner	1 2 3 4 5 6 7 8 9 10

2. Jesus alive again – the forecast

Read Mark 10:32-34

What did Jesus tell his disciples about his death?

He would be arrested, sentenced to death, humiliated, bullied and executed by the Romans. He would come alive again three days later.

How would you react if you were a disciple and heard Jesus predict his death?

....

....

....

....

....

Mini-Dictionary

Disciple
One of the people chosen to follow Jesus. Although there were many disciples of Jesus, he had a special team of twelve. These days Christians often call themselves 'disciples' because they're learning to follow Jesus.

Resurrection
When someone comes back to life from death. This is not resuscitation or reincarnation!

8

3. Jesus alive again
— the facts

Read Mark 16:1-8

Briefly describe what happened when Jesus was raised to life.

When Jesus' friends arrived to attend to his body they found the huge boulder blocking the tomb's entrance rolled away. A stranger (an angel) inside told them Jesus was alive. They were scared and confused.

How would you feel if you had discovered Jesus' empty tomb — a grave carved out of a rock in the side of a hill?

. . . .

. . . .

. . . .

. . . .

. . . .

4. Jesus alive again
— what it means

Read Acts 10:39-43

One day after Jesus left the earth, Peter — one of his followers — was talking about him to a Roman army captain called Cornelius. During the conversation, Peter said:

`Jesus was put to death on a cross. But three days later, God raised him to life and let him be seen. Not everyone saw him. He was seen only by us, who ate and drank with him after he was raised from death. We were the ones God chose to tell others about him.

God told us to announce clearly to the people that Jesus is the one he has chosen to judge the living and the dead. Every one of the prophets has said that all who have faith in Jesus will have their sins forgiven in his name.' (Acts 10:39-43)

According to Peter, what will happen to the living and the dead?

All will be judged by Jesus.

Why was it so important for us to have faith in Jesus who rose from the dead?

So that our sins can be forgiven.

Does this suggest we are free to do whatever we want in our lives? If not, why not?

We can do what we like, but we will be judged by Christ.

9

6. The resurrection is of vital importance. Because Jesus rose from death, we can be certain that we will rise from death one day. But we can also be certain that we will be judged. Jesus is the judge!

7. It is uncomfortable to talk about divisions. It seems intolerant. But this is clearly the message of the Bible. God certainly does not throw people out without giving them a good chance. So the matter is in our hands. Being rescued from punishment is not automatic. We have important choices to make. People who turn their backs on God are saying: 'I don't need Jesus. I'll look after myself. Things will turn out OK in the end.' But these Bible verses show us that 'in the end' we have to answer the charges against us and only Jesus can acquit us.

8. Invite the group to continue reading Mark's Gospel. The section for this week is chapters 10-13.

5. Jesus alive again – so what?

Read Mark 8:38 and 2 Thessalonians 1:9-10

Paul – a leader of the church – wrote many letters to the groups of followers of Jesus who were scattered around the countries of southern Europe. In one letter, he encouraged those who were under great pressure because of their faith. Things will be different one day, he wrote!

'Our Lord Jesus Christ will punish anyone who doesn't know God and won't obey his message. Their punishment will be eternal destruction, and they will be kept far from the presence of our Lord and his glorious strength. This will happen on that day when the Lord returns to be praised and honoured by all who have faith in him and belong to him. This includes you, because you believed what we said.'
(2 Thessalonians 1:8-10)

What will happen to those people who have turned their backs on Jesus?

Punishment, destruction and separation
from God.

What about those who believe in Jesus?
What do these verses tell us?

With Jesus giving praise and honour.

10

good enough?

AIM

To show that we can never achieve God's approval through efforts of our own. It is God's grace and love which offers us rescue from punishment for our sin.

SESSION NOTES

1. Allow time for questions arising from Mark 10-16. The common questions raised in these chapters are covered in the 'Top Twenty' section on pages 41-48.

2. The opening exercise involves the group members writing their own obituary. There are no right or wrong responses to this and they may not wish to share what they wrote.

   Invite the group to think about what God's assessment might be. Just pose the question and leave it hanging at this stage.

3. Then invite the group to write 'Yes, No or Maybe' alongside the statements in Panel 2. Again, no need to share these in the group.

   Activities and achievements like these are commonly called 'good works' in the Bible.

   A helpful explanation of this is outlined on page 29, 'My Stairway to Heaven'. This would be a good time to use the first part of this explanation — Envelope No. 1.

4. Invite the group to read Mark 7:20-23 and fill in the questions. If members do not have full New Testaments, print Romans 3:23 and 6:23 on pieces of card so that all questions can be answered.

5. Read the bandaid story in the workbook and talk over how it connects with our relationship with God.

6. Continue with the explanation 'My Stairway to Heaven' on page 29. Talk about the second envelope.

continued page 28.

good enough?

SESSION D

1. Do-it-yourself funerals.

We all have to die at some point. What sort of things would you want said about you at your funeral? What might your friends, family, work mates remember about you and your achievements? Write them down.

. . . .

. . . .

. . . .

. . . .

Would God's list be the same? Why or why not? What does God see as important in your character and achievements?

. . . .

. . . .

2. How important are the following activities for getting a ticket to heaven?
(Write *Yes*, *No* or *Maybe* after each.)

- Collecting money for the Salvation Army?
- Going to church on Sundays?
- Helping old ladies to cross streets?
- Doing whatever your parents ask?
- Obtaining top marks at school?

3. What I have done!
Read Mark 7:20-23

What things make a person unclean?

Evil thoughts, vulgar deeds, stealing, murder, unfaithfulness in marriage, greed, meanness, deceit, indecency, envy, insults, pride, foolishness.

Where do these come from?

From the heart — from bad attitudes.

What is God's standard for everyone? Can anyone reach God's standard? Read Romans 3:21-24.

Good attitudes resulting in good deeds, but only faith in Jesus can make this happen.

So, what is the penalty for our sin? Read Romans 6:23.

Everyone fails.

4. What is important to God?

- Spending time with him?
- Knowing God's character?
- Patterning your life on Jesus?
- Knowing that Jesus died for your sins?
- Believing you are acceptable to him?

11

6. Check-up time

Suppose you go to the doctor with red spots over your body, and you are told you've got measles. Imagine the doctor then tried to cure you by putting bandaids over each of the spots! You would say 'Hold on, the spots are only the symptoms. The real disease is inside. It's in my blood stream!' So it is with sin. When we do say or think wrong things these are only the symptom of sin, the real problem is within. The Bible says our hearts are in rebellion against God, either actively or passively. Doing a few good deeds is just 'bandaiding' the problem or covering it up. The central problem is that we each want to ignore God and run our lives our own way.

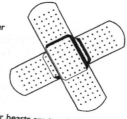

7. What Christ has done

Read Ephesians 2:1-10

Is 'grace' just a girl's name?

If we can't be saved by our own good deeds and achievements, what can save us? (Ephesians 2:8-9, Romans 5:8)

Believing that Christ died for us despite what we are like.

The word grace means a free gift which is totally undeserved. Can you think of an example of that kind of gift? (Maybe a gift you received?)

Birthday gifts, encouragement awards, courtesy gestures, being 'shouted' a drink or a meal etc.

What does verse 8 now mean?

God rescued us from our sin even though we did not deserve this.

Imagine you are climbing a stairway to heaven. How are you going to talk your way in at the door? What would you say?

When does a gift become a gift?

When it is accepted.

What place in our lives do good works have?

God didn't rescue us because of our good works; they are our way of saying thankyou.

12

7. If your group does not have sufficient New Testaments, photocopy Ephesians 2:1-10 and distribute them to the group. (You have permission from the Bible Society to copy only these verses in either the *Good News Bible* or the *Contemporary English Version*. Be sure to add a note to the foot of the sheet identifying the version and indicating that it is copied with permission. Note this permission does not apply to other versions.)

8. Invite group members to think seriously about the THINK ABOUT idea at the end.

9. Encourage the group members to read chapters 14–16 from Mark's Gospel before the next session.

my stairway to heaven

This is an attempt to explain visually the deal between God and us. It comes from *Christianity Explained* by the Rev. Michael Bennett, published by SU Queensland. It fits at point 3 in the session notes of Session D.

THE ENVELOPES

Envelope number 1 (I suggest 305mm x 155mm envelope) has a large X on the back, and on the front in bold print, the words **'I earned God's forgiveness because of my good life and achievements.'** Inside this envelope is another smaller envelope (I suggest a 235 x 120mm manilla envelope). This envelope has the words WHAT I HAVE DONE printed on the front in bold letters, with the word **I** emphasised. Inside this envelope are a number of cards with these words, each on a different card:

My good works; Keeping Ten Commandments; Not killing; Not lying; Not stealing; Good citizen; Bible reading; Gifts to charities; High marks in school; My achievements.

Envelope number 2 has a large tick on the back and on the front, in bold print, the words **'I receive God's forgiveness because he generously and freely offers it.'**

Inside this envelope is a smaller envelope as before, with the words WHAT CHRIST HAS DONE printed on the front in bold letters, with the word CHRIST emphasised. Inside this envelope is the completed diagram of the stool from page 13.

Explain that there are basically only two answers to the question. One is wrong and the other is right.

The wrong answer: What I have done

We are going to look at the wrong answer first. Show the envelope with the cross on the back. Then show the words on the front. Open this envelope and produce the smaller inner envelope: WHAT I HAVE DONE. Open this smaller envelope and show the cards inside, one at a time.

Explain that this is how people try to get right with God. But none of these good works individually, or all of them collectively, can qualify us for heaven.

The right answer: What Christ has done

Show the tick on the back of the other envelope, then the front.

Ask: What do we mean by grace?

Explain that this means an undeserved free gift. Take out the smaller envelope to show the words, WHAT CHRIST HAS DONE. Open this smaller envelope to show the stool diagram. This shows what Christ has done *on our behalf*. (Ephesians 2:8-10)

Explain that it is grace through faith alone that saves us. This salvation is the gift of God. Lay side by side the two smaller envelopes, contrasting WHAT I HAVE DONE with WHAT CHRIST HAS DONE. Explain that it is Christ alone who saves us. We must respond to his love and his death on the cross, by faith.

THE WRONG ANSWER

BACK

I earned God's forgiveness because of **my good life and achievements**. → **WHAT I HAVE DONE** → **MY GOOD WORKS**

FRONT

THE RIGHT ANSWER

BACK

I receive God's forgiveness because he generously and freely offers it. → **WHAT CHRIST HAS DONE** →

FRONT

GUARANTEED

JESUS SAID HE WAS GOD'S SON — THE ORIGINAL AND ONLY GENUINE 'GOD-MAN'.

JESUS PROVED HIS POINT BY COMING ALIVE AGAIN AFTER DYING.

JESUS SHOWED HIS LOVE BY ALLOWING HIMSELF TO BE EXECUTED.

STOOL ILLUSTRATION

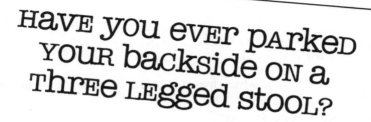

Have you ever parked your backside on a three legged stool?

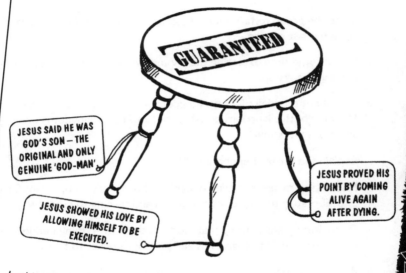

GUARANTEED

JESUS SAID HE WAS GOD'S SON — THE ORIGINAL AND ONLY GENUINE 'GOD-MAN'.

JESUS SHOWED HIS LOVE BY ALLOWING HIMSELF TO BE EXECUTED.

JESUS PROVED HIS POINT BY COMING ALIVE AGAIN AFTER DYING.

In this story three legs is important!

Four legs is boring, and

two legs is very shaky indeed.

Try this three legged stool for size!

It won't let you down.

Faith is trusting something that won't let you down.

Blind faith is trusting something you haven't checked.

What are you relying on? Will it hold you safely?

13

WHO'S SORRY NOW?

AIM

To understand what it means to repent of the wrong things in our lives.

SESSION NOTES

1. Invite the group to talk about the chapters of Mark they have read since the last session.

2. Spend some time exploring the TV interviewer scenario, comparing ideas in the group.

3. Talk about the idea of God's Kingdom — where God's in charge. How might this kingdom be different from other kingdoms or situations we know?

   Explain the terms 'Repent' and 'Believe'.

   Repenting means changing our mind about what is important for us ... deliberately turning our back on sin and turning to God's way.

   Believing means trusting that God has done everything needed to rescue us from sin, forgives us and gives us a ticket to heaven.

4. Remind the group that following Jesus is not a picnic. It takes decisions of our will every day. Some of these may be easy but some will require determination and guts.

5. Brainstorm about the pain and the gains as listed in Mark 8:34-38. Talk about some possible practical aspects.

6. Using the Bible work on this page talk about the things that stop us from putting Christ in No. 1 spot. Remind the group members that our decisions about following Jesus faithfully have to be renewed and confirmed day after day.

continued page 35.

WHO'S SORRY NOW?

1. Street wisdom

If you were a TV interviewer and went into the streets and asked people, 'In your opinion what is a Christian?', what answers might you get?

....

....

2. So, what is a Christian?

Read Mark 1:15

Why do you think the news was 'good news'?

Because God took the first step to forgive people's sins and invite them to his kingdom.

If there's a kingdom, who's the king?

Jesus Christ.

To become a Christian you need to do two things (verse 15). What are they?

1. Turn back to God

2. Believe the good news.

3. And what's the cost?

What is the toughest thing you were ever asked to do?

....

How did you feel before you attempted it?

....

And after?

....

Mark 8:34-38 is probably the toughest thing Jesus ever asked of his followers. Read it now.

Someone carrying a Roman cross was certainly not in charge of things. As a prisoner being ordered about by soldiers he would not expect soft treatment. It's tough. Not for wimps. You wouldn't choose it. Not actually a picnic! Jesus invites us to choose something like this every day.

What do you think Jesus meant when he said, 'If you want to be my followers, you must forget about yourself. You must take up your cross and follow me'?

To put God's preferences ahead of mine.

Think again about Mark 8:34-38 and imagine Jesus saying the words to you, today. Try to write down some examples of the pain and the gains.

PAIN	GAINS
Hardship	*Jesus accepts me*
Give up preferences	*Saved life*
Stick with Jesus	*Rescue by God*
Don't give up	*Celebrate God's glory*

In what ways in your life do you try to 'own the whole world'? Can these things have a part in your life if Jesus is No. 1?

What do you think people (family, friends) would think of you if you put Jesus first in your life?

But more than anything else, put God's work first and do what he wants. Then the other things will be yours as well. (Matthew 6:33)

14

4. Tough words

Read Mark 9:43-48

Are these verses telling us to cut off our limbs?

No! Obeying Jesus is serious.

Don't lead others astray.

5. Jesus No. 1?

What sort of things could prevent people from putting Jesus No.1?

Pride, peer pressure, popularity, fear.

If something or someone were stopping you from putting Jesus first, what should you do about it?

Remove it; regularly check Jesus is still No. 1.

 Does it seem too easy to just accept salvation as a gift? Is it just pride stopping me from submitting my life to Jesus?

6. Take a deep breath

Read Mark 10:29-31

If following Jesus costs us 'people' or 'things' in this life what does Jesus say will happen?

God's rewards will come.

At the end of this life what does Jesus promise?

Life that lasts forever.

7. So, what do I get?

What gifts does God promise to those who repent and believe?

Mark 1:8   *The Holy Spirit.*

Mark 2:10   *Forgiveness.*

Mark 10:30   *Everlasting life.*

15

7. Explain how a person might make a commitment to become a Christian. To assist this brief explanation, you might find one of the summaries useful.

THANK YOU
for your love
SORRY
for my sin
PLEASE
forgive me and
take over my life

TURN
to God
TRUST
Jesus
TRAVEL
Jesus' way

Encourage group members to think seriously about this step without pressure, invite them to speak with you if they need help. If they decide to take this step of faith, urge them to speak to you for advice about how to go on further with Jesus.

8. Encourage group members to read the following passages from Mark's Gospel before the next session. Mark 1:15; 8:34-38; 9:43-48; 10:29-31. Invite them to write down the most important phrases.

SESSION F

true Believer

AIM

To explain what faith in God is all about, showing that repenting, believing, trusting are action words.

SESSION NOTES

1. Compare notes between group members from the passages from Mark that they read between sessions.

2. Warm up with the 'never trust anyone' exercise. Compare ideas. Talk about trust being active.

3. Think about the story of Jairus. When thinking about Jairus' feelings about the death of his daughter, refer to the train illustration on page 19 of the participants' book.

4. Talk about faith. Try to show that this is something we exercise every day in all sorts of ordinary ways. Show how it is not so much the quantity or **size** of our faith but **who** we have faith in. Talk about the faith of the woman who touched Jesus' coat seeking healing from a very embarrassing illness. Her faith was certainly large enough to believe that Jesus could do it. It would have cost her greatly to slip through the crowd to get that close to Jesus. She would have felt she was an outcast who might be pushing her luck far too much. Some could say that in her vulnerability, healing would have seemed too good to be true – hence her embarrassment and fear about being 'outed'. Refer to the little stool on page 13. Which is the more important: to put a lot of faith in a weak stool or a little faith in a strongly built stool? Make no mistake, a weak stool will still let you down no matter how sincere your faith is!

5. The story of Blondin, allegedly a true story, is a fine example of active faith. (See page 18.) Show that faith is active – it is based on what I know about Jesus. I know he is capable of rescuing and forgiving me. I trust he will do what he promises. I will therefore take action and let Jesus be the Boss of my life. Remind group members of your willingness to chat with them if they want help to take their first steps of faith in Christ.

SESSION F true Believer

1. 'Never trust anyone over thirty' used to be a popular slogan.

How would you re-write that?

Never trust anyone who

....

'Never trust anyone'? Name a person you trust completely and state why you do.

....

Think privately of a person you do not trust. Don't name the person, but say why do you not trust him or her.

....

Complete this sentence:
If my friend double-crossed me or lied behind my back, I would

....

2. Faith – alive

Read Mark 5:21-24, 35-43

How do you think Jairus felt when the message came, 'Your daughter is dead'.

Frustrated, devastated, angry at the woman who delayed Jesus.

What did Jairus do even when he had received this message ?

He kept hanging on in faith.

16

3. Faith – quantity

Read Mark 5:25-34

How did the woman believe she could be healed? (verse 28)

By taking an active faith step of touching Jesus' coat.

Do you think the woman's faith was large or small?

Difficult – see point 4 in session notes.

Which is most effective ...

- to put a lot of faith in a weak chair, or,
  - a little faith in a strong chair?

4. Faith direction

People have faith in all different things. For example, we have faith that the dentist will cure our toothache!

What are some other things in which people put their faith?

Medicine, ladders, team coaches, abseiling ropes, professional advice, etc.

In who or what did the woman have faith? (verse 28)

Jesus.

Where should a Christian place their faith?

In Christ and his capacity to forgive us, to lead us to God and to make us part of his team.

5. Faith openness

Why did Jesus want the person who touched him to come forward? (verse 30)

To help the woman make her faith more active and open. So he could help her and encourage her.

What are some ways you can show openly that your faith and trust is in Jesus? Read Hebrews 10:23-25

Encouraging other Christians, supporting each other to obey Jesus, meeting regularly to worship.

Which is most important – 'FAITH in Jesus', or 'faith in JESUS'?

Am I ready to jump in?

17

Blondin was a famous stunt artist in America. Many years ago he stretched a wire rope across the top of Niagara Falls and walked across it.

Next he announced that he was going to wheel a man in a wheelbarrow across the wire. A newspaper reporter came to interview Blondin about his proposed stunt.

'Do you think I can do this great feat?', Blondin asked the reporter.

'I really believe you can', he replied.

'You believe I can do it?', Blondin asked again. 'Well then you get in the wheelbarrow!'

18

shunt off Thomas!

When you were a little kid, you may have had a train set or loved the stories of Thomas the tank engine. We can learn something valuable from a simple toy train. It doesn't explain everything, but it helps.

The train will run with or without the caboose. However it would be stupid to try to pull the loco by the caboose. That's a bit like a healthy Christian life. It is important to listen to your feelings. If you're feeling uneasy about something, then it's a good idea to stop and seriously think things over. That's when it's good to get things in the right order. However, we do not finally determine if God is working in our lives by how we feel.

One thing's for sure, feelings come and go. They can be affected by what we eat, how much sleep we got last night, what our best friend said over lunch. So our feelings have to be tested. The Bible gives us strong facts about who Jesus was, what he came to do and what he promises. These facts are trustworthy. They are worth relying on. Then let the feelings fall into line. They will if you give them time.

FEELINGS

FAITH

FACTS

mark's gospel: the twenty most asked questions

1. What are evil spirits? Mark 1:23-27

The Bible takes seriously the reality of an unseen spiritual world. This spiritual world has both a good side and an evil or malignant side. The Bible depicts Satan as personal and powerful. His work is totally opposed to God and directed against God's people. Evil spirits (or demons) mentioned in the Gospels are the Devil's agents in this work. Although Satan is immensely powerful, the New Testament shows Jesus to be Lord over Satan, and to have defeated him through his death and resurrection.

2. Why did Jesus tell healed people not to tell anyone? Mark 1:34; 7:36

Jesus did not want to be likened to a side-show with people coming just to see signs and wonders. He rejected such people (Mark 8:11-13; John 4:48). If people did not respond to the preaching of the kingdom of God calling for repentance and faith (Mark 1:15), miracles alone would not convince them. Miracles attract people, and perhaps Jesus saw that the curious crowds would hamper his ministry, as did happen (Mark 1:45).

3. Why did Jesus call himself the Son of Man? Mark 2:10

Jesus wanted to identify with the human race, so he preferred to be called *Son of Man* rather than *Son of God*. *Son of Man* is a Jewish term meaning simply 'a man'.

Son of Man is also a well known title used in the Old Testament for the Messiah (King) God promised to send to Israel (See Daniel 7:13-14). In this vision Daniel saw 'one like a son of man' (i.e. like a human being). God then gives to this son of man an eternal kingdom over all the nations of the earth. The religious leaders in Jesus' day would have understood this code use of *Son of Man* for the coming Messiah, the fulfilment of Daniel's prophecy.

4. New cloth, old clothes; new wine, old skins. Mark 2:21-22

People complained that Jesus did not observe the religious rules and traditions of his day (Mark 2:18). The religious 'heavies' had thousands of laws and religious regulations, and they taught that a person had to strictly observe these to please God. Jesus said that the life he had come to bring was totally incompatible with this system. Jesus could not be 'fitted into' their legalistic religion. He brought a living relationship with God, not rules; grace, love and peace, not religious formulae. Christianity is *not* a religion.

5. What is the 'eternal sin'? Mark 3:29

The key to this is the context. The religious leaders observed Jesus' miracles and heard his teaching at first hand. However, their assessment of Jesus was that he was 'Beelzebul' (Mark 3:22) — an old name for the Devil. They hardened their hearts against the work of God's Spirit through the ministry of Jesus. This unrepentant, continuous attitude is called 'speaking against the Holy Spirit' (Mark 3:29 CEV). This has nothing to do with swearing at the Holy Spirit or 'blaspheming'. In simple terms it means to **continuously** reject Jesus' claim to your life.

For this there was no forgiveness: they refused the only way of forgiveness that God provides. Of course, it is only unforgivable for as long as a person continues to refuse the offer. Many of the religious leaders did repent later on, and so were forgiven (Acts 6:7). This is a vital personal concept. If I reject Jesus, I can *never* be forgiven!

6. Why did Jesus teach in stories (parables)? Mark 4:10-12

Many people have trouble with this passage. On the surface it sounds as if Jesus taught in parables so that people would *not* understand, which is strange indeed. However, two groups are mentioned here: Jesus' followers, often known as 'disciples', and 'those outside'. The disciples were intrigued by the parables and drew nearer to Jesus to hear the explanation. There is a spiritual principle here — 'to those who have more will be given'.

However, to 'those outside' who blocked their ears to Jesus' teaching, the parables remained baffling stories. Their spiritual interest was not aroused. They 'hear, but do not understand'. People are either attracted to the light of Jesus' teaching or repelled by it. Jesus' words, including his parables, always act in this two-fold way. (See also Mark 4:33-34.)

7. Did Jesus have brothers and sisters? Mark 6:3

This passage mentions four brothers by name and at least two sisters. These were presumably the natural children of Joseph and Mary conceived after the birth of Jesus. (See also Mark 3:32.) Some Christians hold that Mary remained a virgin after the birth of Jesus, and that the brothers and sisters mentioned here are really cousins. The Greek word *adelphoi* can also mean 'cousins'. However, Matthew 1:25 seems to imply that Joseph and Mary entered into a normal sexual relationship after Jesus' birth.

8. Throwing the children's food to the dogs? Mark 7:24-30

The key to this difficult passage is that the woman was not a Jew; she was a Greek speaking Phoenician. Jesus' ministry at this stage was exclusively to the Jews, the descendants of Abraham. His strategy at this period was not to preach to the foreigners (Gentiles) nor Israel's neighbours, the Samaritans (Matt. 10:5).

Jesus says to her, 'The children must first be fed! It isn't right to take away their food and feed it to dogs!' The term 'children' here refers to the Jews while 'dogs' was a common, unflattering expression for foreigners. So Jesus is saying: 'It isn't right to take what belongs to the Jews and give it to you foreigners.'

In her reply (verse 28) the woman is really saying, 'Yes Lord — I acknowledge that as a foreign woman I have no claim upon you, the Jewish Messiah. But at least give me a few moments of your time to deal with a problem I have!' Jesus is impressed by her faith and her persistence and grants her request (Matt. 15:28).

9. What is the 'yeast of the Pharisees and of Herod'? Mark 8:15

'Yeast' means influence. Just as a tiny amount of yeast has a large effect on the whole batch of dough, so Jesus warns against the 'yeast' of people like King Herod and the Pharisee religious leaders. Though few in number, the Pharisees were the most influential religious party in Jesus' day. They taught that rigorous law-keeping was the path to God. Jesus called them 'hypocrites' (the word means 'play-actors') for their public displays of religion and self-righteousness.

A writer has said, 'The yeast of Herod is adultery, murder, hastiness in swearing, affectation in piety and hatred of Christ and his forerunner

(John the Baptist).' So, Jesus is warning against outward religious show (the Pharisees) and crass worldliness (Herod).

10. 'Don't you know what I am talking about by now?' Mark 8:17-21

Twice Jesus fed large crowds of Jewish people in a desert place where no food was available. As Jews, this would have reminded them of the way God fed the people of Israel in the desert, when led there by Moses. God gave them 'manna' food. They would also have remembered Moses' prophecy, made towards the end of his life: '(God) will choose one of your own people to be a prophet just like me' (Deut. 18:15). Yet still the disciples did not understand that Jesus was the prophet predicted by Moses, the expected Messiah. It is no accident that in the very next section Peter declares; 'You are the Messiah' (Mark 8:29). The penny has dropped, at last!

11. What is 'God's kingdom come with power'? Mark 9:1

This is probably a reference to the coming of the Holy Spirit on the day of Pentecost. After his resurrection Jesus said to his disciples: 'But the Holy Spirit will come upon you and give power' (Acts 1:8). The kingdom of God *came* with the entry of Jesus into the world. It *came with power* at the pouring out of God the Holy Spirit.

12. Who is Elijah? Mark 9:11-13

In the last statement of the Old Testament, God promised that he would send again Elijah the prophet before the day of the Lord! (Malachi 4:5-6) Elijah was a prophet in the 8th century BC. He dressed in a distinctive way, wearing animal skins and a leather belt (2 Kings 1:8). When John the Baptist appeared he dressed in a similar manner (Matt. 3:4). Jesus makes it clear that John was the fulfilment of the prophecy concerning Elijah.

Does this mean that John was a prophet like Elijah, or that John was Elijah come back to life again? Probably the former, though it is not clear from the Gospels.

13. What does it mean to cut off your hand, etc? Mark 9:43-48

Jesus obviously did not intend that a Christian should physically cut off a hand or foot, or pluck out an eye! In this dramatic way, Jesus is saying that if anything is stopping you from entering the kingdom of God, it is better to take drastic and perhaps sacrificial action to rid yourself of that obstacle, rather than to end up totally out of touch with God. The logic is obvious: temporary pain is a better option! Jesus often offered people stark choices.

14. Divorce — what does Jesus say? Mark 10:1-12

Jesus makes it clear that divorce is always against God's ideal for faithful relationships. God's plan, since creation, is that married people should live together for the whole of their lives (verses 6-9). This is God's ideal. Jesus also emphasised that if people divorce just because they have found a nicer partner, such action is adultery (verses 11-12).

Divorce has always occurred because people's hearts can become hard (verse 5). Some think that divorce is an unforgivable sin, but Christ came to die for all sin, including any sin associated with divorce. In talking to the Samaritan woman in John chapter 4, Jesus knew that she had already been divorced five times and was now living with a sixth man. Some responsibility for the failure of these marriages must lie with the woman, but knowing these facts, Jesus still freely offered her acceptance and forgiveness. 'You don't know what God wants to give you, and you don't know who is asking you for a drink. If you did, you would ask me for the water that gives life.' (John 4:10)

It is not our role to be moral police. Like Jesus, we must freely hold out the water of forgiveness, cleansing and eternal life. If the subject of divorce becomes a major issue in your *Cross Examination* group, it may be advisable to arrange an extra session, and involve a minister or counsellor who can helpfully explain Christian teaching on this.

15. Why did Jesus curse the fig tree? Mark 11:12-14, 20-25

This action has perplexed many Christians. It was Jesus' only destructive miracle. Here are two possible explanations:

(a)   Jesus was teaching his disciples about the power of prayer. Certainly that was the interpretation that Jesus himself gave in the following verses (verses 22-24), saying in effect, 'This power is available to you too. If you say to this hill ... etc.'

(b)   Many commentators have suggested that this is an *acted parable*, a parable without words! Many such acted parables were used by the Old Testament prophets. Jesus went to the Temple (verse 11). It should have been the most spiritual place on earth, but when Jesus looked around the place he saw only spiritual bankruptcy – a commercial racket going on.

The next day he cleansed the Temple (verses 15-19). Wedged between these two incidents — Jesus' observation of Temple life and his cleansing of the Temple — is his cursing of the fig tree. Some suggest that the fig tree refers to the religious leaders of Israel. Instead of finding spiritual fruitfulness in the Temple, he found barrenness, like the fig tree. Just as the tree was cursed, so too Israel would come under God's disapproval for her spiritual emptiness.

This idea of the coming destruction of the Temple is taken up more fully in chapter 13. Both Temple and the city of Jerusalem were destroyed by the Roman armies in AD 70, about 37 years later.

16. One bride for seven brothers? Mark 12:18-27

What is the point of this trick question? In Jesus' day there were two major religious parties: the *Pharisees,* who believed in life after death, and the *Sadducees*, who said that death was the end — there was no hope of life beyond the grave, or resurrection (verse 18).

The Sadducees thus came up with this question (verses 18-23). In his answer to them in verses 24-27 Jesus says two things:

• There is life beyond the grave, but no marriage relationship as such. This does not mean that married couples will not know each other in heaven — just that sexual relationships will have ended.

• God did not say, 'I *was* the God of Abraham, Isaac, Jacob ...' but, 'I *am* the God worshipped by Abraham ... '. I am still their God, because they live on! The hope of the resurrection is the central Christian hope.

17. What is the 'Horrible Thing'? Mark 13:14

A parallel passage in Luke's Gospel, gives the key to the mystery of the 'Horrible Thing'. Luke chapter 21 parallels Mark chapter 13. Luke tends to explain difficult words or expressions. In place of Mark 13:14, Luke has these words; 'When you see Jerusalem surrounded by soldiers ... if you are living in Judea at that time, run to the mountains' (Luke 21:20-21).

So in place of the 'Horrible Thing', Luke has 'Jerusalem surrounded by soldiers'.

In AD 65 the Roman armies, surrounded Jerusalem following a political uprising. After a terrible five-year war, the Roman armies entered the city, desecrated the Holy of Holies in the Temple, then proceeded to pull down both the Temple and the city. So Jesus' words in Mark chapter 13 did come to pass.

18. Why did Jesus not know the date of his own return? Mark 13:32

Some people have suggested that, because Jesus did not know the date of his own return, this made him less than perfect, less than divine. So, since God is omniscient (knows everything), Jesus cannot be God.

Two comments need to be made:

* There is a great mystery here. 'When he became like one of us', Jesus 'gave up everything' (Phil. 2:7). As a baby and child, Jesus had to grow in wisdom, as all human children do. He was not born with a complete built-in knowledge. Jesus would most likely not have known anything about computers, ball point pens or fuel injected car engines.

* It is not sinful to lack knowledge. It is sinful to make dogmatic statements on the basis of little or no real knowledge. Jesus freely acknowledged that he did not know the date of his return.

If Jesus did not know, why should we speculate! This is one little touch which verifies the truth of the Bible. If someone had made up the story of Jesus Christ, they would have left out Mark 13:32.

19. Was the darkness an eclipse? Mark 15:33

It has been suggested that the darkness over the cross of Jesus was caused by a daytime eclipse of the sun. However, this is not possible. Jesus was crucified at the time of the Jewish Passover, which is always at full moon. Then the heavenly bodies are in an almost straight line: Sun — Earth — Moon. To have a daytime eclipse of the sun the bodies must be in an exact straight line: Sun — Moon — Earth.

Physically, we cannot find an adequate explanation for this account of darkness. Yet it appears to be in keeping with humanity's darkest deed!

20. Why are there odd endings to Mark's Gospel? Mark chapter 16

Most scholars agree that Mark's Gospel ends abruptly at verse 8 in a rather unsatisfactory manner. The women have seen the empty tomb and been informed of the resurrection of Jesus, but there is no account of Jesus appearing, as in the other three Gospels.

The additional endings of Mark's Gospel appear to be attempts by well-meaning scribes to add some resurrection appearances to Mark. However, the style of the original Greek changes from verse 8 onwards. This does not mean that the material from verses 9 to the end is wrong or fictional, for many of the details can be double-checked from the other Gospels. It just means that they were probably not in Mark's original version.